VAN BU
DECA   W9-AFT-015

In Memory of

Genevieve Ewert

© DEMCO, INC. 1990 PRINTED IN U.S.A.

Trumpets

Music Makers

T H E C H I L D ' S W O R L D®, I N C.

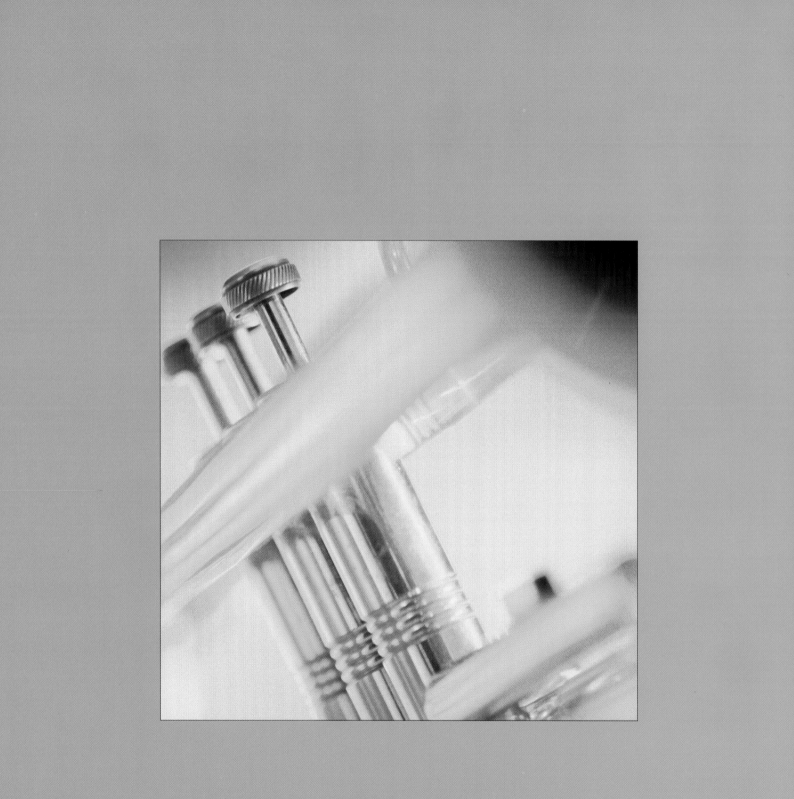

Trumpets

Pamela K. Harris

THE CHILD'S WORLD®, INC.

J
788.921
Har

Copyright © 2001 by The Child's World®, Inc.
All rights reserved. No part of this book may be
reproduced or utilized in any form or by any means
without written permission from the publisher.
Printed in the United States of America.

Library of Congress Cataloging-in-Publication Data
Harris, Pamela K., 1962–
Trumpets / by Pamela K. Harris.
p. cm.
Includes index.
Summary: Simple text describes the parts of a trumpet,
the history of the instrument, and how it is played.
ISBN 1-56766-680-9 (lib. reinforced. : alk. paper)
1. Trumpet—Juvenile literature. [1. Trumpet.] I. Title.
ML960 .H37 2000
788.9'219—dc21   00-020607

Credits

Translation: Neil Carruthers,
University of Canterbury, Christchurch, New Zealand
Graphic design: Brad Clemmons

Photo Credits

© www.comstock.com: cover, 3, back cover
© PhotoDisc: 12, 14, 17, 19, 23
© Stone/Donna Day: 6; Anthony Cassidy: 8; Tom Raymond: 11;
   Ernest Haas: 20

Table of Contents

Chapter	Page
The Trumpet	6
Different Kinds of Trumpets	9
Brass Instruments	10
The Shape	13
Parts of a Trumpet	15
Playing the Trumpet	16
The Valves	18
Jazz Trumpet	21
Sounds of the Trumpet	22
Other Brass Instruments	23
Glossary and Index	24

The Trumpet

The king is coming! The king is coming! Trumpets blare the news. Long ago, trumpets were played for kings and queens. Their special sound grew to be loved by almost everyone who heard it.

The sound of a trumpet is still loved today. Instead of just being played for kings and queens, trumpets are played almost everywhere. Trumpets belong to a group of instruments called **wind instruments**. Wind instruments make sounds when air is blown through them. Flutes and trombones are wind instruments, too.

Trumpets can make very loud music! →

Different Kinds of Trumpets

Trumpets are very old instruments. In fact, some trumpets were even discovered in a pyramid in Egypt! One trumpet was made of silver. Another was made of bronze.

Long ago, most trumpets were made from reeds, horns, or shells. Since they could make such loud noises, trumpets were often used for celebrations. Today, most trumpets are made of brass.

← This man is playing a trumpet during a celebration.

Brass Instruments

There are two types of instruments in the wind instrument group. **Woodwinds** have lots of holes that musicians must open and close with their fingertips. Covering each hole changes the woodwind's sound.

Brass instruments are usually made of metal. They have **valves** to move the air in different directions. This changes the instrument's sound. Some brass instruments have parts that slide in and out to change the sound. Trumpets belong to the brass group.

How many trumpets can you see in this picture? →

The Shape

Trumpets from long ago looked very different from the ones we know today. The oldest trumpets were just a straight tube that widened at the end. These instruments were very long and heavy. People had to rest one end on the ground to play them!

To make trumpets easier to play, instrument makers began to bend the tube of the trumpet. Over time, the tube became even more curved. Today, the tube part of a trumpet looks like a flattened letter "S."

← The end of a trumpet looks like a bell.

mouthpiece

valves

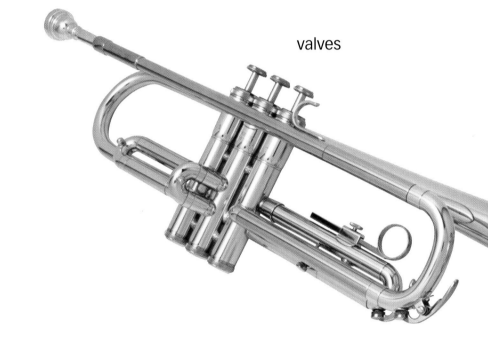

bell

straight mute

cup mute

Parts of a Trumpet

A trumpet is a hollow tube with a **mouthpiece** on one end and a flared **bell** on the other. The bell makes the sound louder—like cupping your hands around your mouth. Sometimes the bell end is blocked with a *mute*. The mute changes the **volume** and **tone** of the sounds the trumpet makes. It makes the trumpet play quieter and with a softer sound.

Playing the Trumpet

To play a trumpet, you put your lips on the mouthpiece and make them **vibrate** as you blow. You have to blow so that the air goes into the tube. Don't let any air escape from the sides of your mouth!

This trumpet player is blowing air into the mouthpiece. ➜

The Valves

Valves change the sounds or notes a trumpet can make. Pushing a valve down forces the air through a side tube. It travels around, comes back through the main tube, and goes out through the bell. Making the air travel around—rather than directly through the bell—changes the sound. This is how a trumpet makes different notes.

The valves move up and down to make different notes. →

The trumpet is often played in *jazz music*. Louis Armstrong was one of the greatest trumpet players of all time. He was one of the first jazz trumpeters to play **solo,** or by himself.

Sounds of the Trumpet

Trumpets are played in all kinds of music. You can hear them played in orchestras, rock groups, and dance bands. You have probably seen them in marching bands, too. Would you like to play the trumpet?

Other Brass Instruments

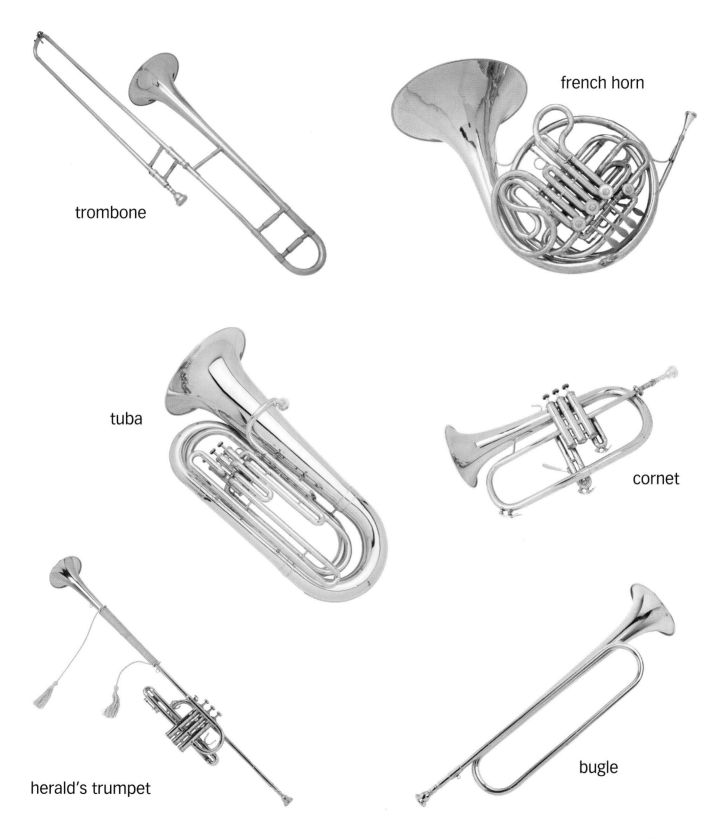

trombone

french horn

tuba

cornet

herald's trumpet

bugle

Glossary

bell (BELL)
A bell is the flared end of a trumpet. The bell makes the trumpet's sound louder.

brass instruments (BRASS IN-struh-mentz)
Brass instruments are played by blowing air through a tube, then pressing down valves or moving a slide. Trumpets are brass instruments.

mouthpiece (MOWTH-peese)
The mouthpiece of a trumpet is where you put your mouth. Blowing air through the mouthpiece creates the trumpet's sound.

solo (SOH-loh)
When a musician plays solo, he or she plays all alone.

tone (TOHN)
Tone is how a note sounds. Trumpets can make many kinds of tones, like a sad tone or a happy tone.

valves (VALVZ)
The valves on a trumpet change the notes the trumpet plays. Pressing down on a valve forces the air inside the trumpet into a side tube.

vibrate (VY-brayt)
When something vibrates, it moves back and forth. To play a trumpet, you vibrate your lips on the mouthpiece.

volume (VAHL-yoom)
Volume is how loud or quiet a sound is. Trumpets can play at a very high volume.

wind instruments (WIND IN–struh-ments)
Wind instruments are instruments that need to have air blown into them to make a sound. Trumpets are wind instruments.

woodwinds (WOOD-windz)
Woodwinds are tube-shaped instruments that are played by blowing air into a mouthpiece. Clarinets and flutes are woodwinds.

Index

Armstrong, Louis, 21
bell, 15, 18
brass instruments, 10
jazz music, 21
mouthpiece, 15
mute, 15
playing, 16
shape, 13, 15
solo, 21
sound, 6, 9, 10, 15, 18
tone, 15
tube, 13, 16, 18
valves, 10, 18
vibrate, 16
volume, 15
wind instruments, 6
woodwinds, 10

DISCARDED

DISCARDED